I0560827

Spooky Action at a Distance

A Comedy in Three Acts

by

Stephen Evans

For my Angel.

This is a work of fiction. The names, characters, places, and incidents are either the products of the author's imagination or are used fictitiously, and any resemblance to actual persons living or dead, business establishments, events, or locales is entirely coincidental.

For production permissions and other information, please contact Time Being Media LLC at:

info@TimeBeingMedia.com.

Copyright © 2024 by Stephen Evans. All rights reserved.

Book Layout ©2017 BookDesignTemplates.com

Spooky Action at a Distance: Stephen Evans, Fourth Edition

ISBN: 978-1953725714

 Time Being Media LLC

"God does not play dice with the Universe."

Albert Einstein

"The dice of God are always loaded."

Ralph Waldo Emerson

STEPHEN EVANS

Cast of Characters

HAROLD: A cosmologist, aging.

Angel: A dancer, ageless.

Scene

A hotel/casino in Las Vegas.

Time

Now.

Act I Scene 1

Setting: A hotel room, not very plush. The room has one queen-size bed, a dresser, a chair, an old television, a mirror.

At Rise: The room is dark, except for a red blinking light seeping through the closed blinds, as though the world's biggest stop light had gone crazy outside.

The door opens. We hear casino bells—down the hall but VERY LOUD.

Harold WILSON stumbles into the room with a suitcase and a large artist's portfolio case. He is dressed in a tuxedo. The door closes behind him but stays slightly ajar.

Harold dumps everything into a jumble on the bed.

HAROLD

Let there be light.

He turns on a lamp, illuminating the room.

Harold removes a marker board and easel from the portfolio case. He sets up the easel and board, which has mathematical equations written on it:

Harold stands back and chuckles.

At the dresser, he empties his pockets, dumping many silver dollars into a cardboard bucket that says Casino Voltaire. He places the suitcase on the dresser and removes a CD player (this could be a phone, or anything that can play music), a bottle of scotch, a bottle of pills, a gun, and a rope tied in a hangman's noose.

He swigs the scotch, and turns on the CD. The 'Of Science and Learning' section of Strauss' Thus Spake Zarathustra fills the room.

Harold shoves the bed under the ceiling fixture. He climbs up and ties the noose to the fixture. Then he climbs down, picks up the gun and the bottle of pills. He struggles to open the pills, finally succeeds, then pours them into his hand. He takes another swig but doesn't swallow, then climbs back on the bed, mouth full, gun in one hand and pills in the other.

He accidentally hits the noose with his head. It swings back and forth. He swings his head back and forth, trying to slip into it, unsuccessfully.

Then he hears a knock at the door.

HAROLD
(through a mouth full of scotch)
Hmm HuHmmm. (Go away).

There's another knock.

HAROLD
Hmm HummmHmmm. (I'm busy).

There is another knock, very insistent.

HAROLD
Hmm HuHmmm HuhHuhHuh. (Go away, God dammit).

The door swings open.

The light in the hallway is blinding. Casino bells blast in.

Angel appears, framed in the doorway, in a very sexy Angel costume with gossamer wings visible behind her, a little bent. Her halo is straight and gleaming.

Harold spits out the scotch.

Drops the pills.

Falls off the bed.

Accidentally squeezes the trigger.

The gun fires.

Angel drops to the floor.

Harold rises.

> HAROLD

Oh my God. I killed an Angel.

He looks up.

> HAROLD

That's not good.

Harold puts the gun down, runs toward Angel, and slips on the pills on the floor.

He picks himself up, shakes his head, remembers what he was doing, runs toward Angel, slips again.

He picks himself up, shakes his head, remembers what he was doing, runs toward her, side steps that area of the floor, and kneels down in the hallway by her side.

He tries to wake her and can't, so he lifts her up, with some difficulty.

> HAROLD

You'd think Angels would be light.

He angles her this way and that, trying to get her wings through the door. Finally he succeeds by standing her up in the doorway, edging inside, and catching her as she falls through.

*A bag or large purse sits next to the door. While
balancing her, he picks it up with his foot and
moves it inside. The door closes shut.*

*Harold takes Angel to the bed and puts her
down. He checks her body for blood. Can't find
any. He listens to her chest.*

*He climbs over her, starts CPR. As he is giving
her mouth-to-mouth resuscitation, her eyes open.*

ANGEL
HuHmmm HuhHuh. (This costs extra).

Harold sits up in shock.

ANGEL
This costs extra.

*Harold realizes his hands are still on her chest
and quickly pulls them off. In a crescendo of
insight, they assert the obvious:*

HAROLD
You're alive.

ANGEL
You shot me.

HAROLD
You're alive.

ANGEL
You shot me.

> HAROLD

You're alive!

> ANGEL

You shot me!

She shoves him off her, stands up on the bed, comes face to face with the noose, and screams.

Harold screams too.

Angel pummels Harold, chasing him off the bed, around the room.

> HAROLD

I'm sorry! I'm sorry!

They retreat to neutral corners.

ANGEL	HAROLD
I don't have any money. You can check my purse. I don't have a purse. Check anything you want. Just don't hurt me.	I didn't mean to. It was an accident. I was up on the bed and the door opened and I fell and the gun went off.

Pause

ANGEL	HAROLD
What?	What?

> ANGEL

Don't hurt me.

HAROLD

I never would.

She reassesses him.

ANGEL

Just stay where you are. Don't come near me.

HAROLD

It was an accident. I was up on the chair with the gun.

He picks up the gun.
and you came in and...you startled me.

ANGEL

Yeah, well, it was mutual.

He goes for the phone.

HAROLD

Do you want me to call a doctor?

ANGEL

No! I'm not hit. Just shook up. I must have fainted.

He hangs up.

HAROLD

The police will be here soon anyway. Someone will have heard the shot.

ANGEL

Not likely. We're next to the casino. Those slot machines have the decibel range of a jumbo jet.

He looks up at the ceiling.

HAROLD

What about cameras? I hear they watch everything in a casino.

ANGEL

Eye in the Sky. That's just in the casino, not in the rooms. Thank God.

She puts her hand to her head.

ANGEL

Maybe I'd better lie down.

She holds out her other hand to him, palm up.

HAROLD

Let me help you.

ANGEL

You want to make me feel better? Give me the gun.

He does.

ANGEL

Thanks.

He tries to help her to the bed. She holds him off.

ANGEL

Stop punctuating my equilibrium.

HAROLD

What?

ANGEL

I can do it.

She tries, sinks down and almost topples over.

She holds out her hand to him, palm down this time.

ANGEL

Help me.

He rushes to her, helps her to the bed. She lays the gun down on the nightstand.

ANGEL

I must have hit my head when I fell.

HAROLD

I'll get some ice.

ANGEL

No, it's—

He throws open the door and rushes out. Casino bells blast in. The door closes automatically, shutting tight this time.

ANGEL

Okay.

She sees the strange equations on the board, chuckles.

There is a knock on the door.

ANGEL

Who is it?

> HAROLD (OS)

It's me.

> *(Pause)*

I forgot my key.

> *(Pause)*

I forgot the ice bucket.

> *(Pause)*

This ice is really cold.

> *She sighs, lifts herself unsteadily off the bed,
> moves to the door, and opens it. He's holding the
> ice in his hands.*

> HAROLD

Here.

> *He puts the ice in her hands.*

> ANGEL

This ice is really cold.

> HAROLD

Wait. I'll get an ice bucket.

> ANGEL

No, it's—

> *He rushes out the door again. The door closes
> shut. She shrugs.*

> ANGEL

Useless.

> *She dumps the ice in an ice bucket on the dresser.
> There's another knock.*

ANGEL

Who is it?

HAROLD (OS)

It's me again.

(Pause)

I still don't have my key.

(Pause)

There aren't any ice buckets out here.

(Pause)

I'd really like to come in.

She shuffles back to the door and opens it.

HAROLD

Thank you.

He spots the ice bucket on the dresser.

HAROLD

I think we have the ice situation under control.

Angel wobbles a bit on her feet.

HAROLD

Sorry. I shouldn't have. Let me.

He holds her arm, assists her to the bed again.

HAROLD

How about a drink?

ANGEL

A drink would be good. No ice!

He pours two, sits on the bed and hands her a glass, keeping one for himself.

She drinks hers down.

Harold can't quite get his drink to his mouth because his hand is shaking. She watches this for a moment, then puts her hands around his to steady him. He takes a sip.

HAROLD

Thanks.

She takes his glass and swallows the rest. She gives it back to him. He refills it.

ANGEL

By the way, happy—

(She pulls a card out of her costume)
birthday.

HAROLD

Thanks. What?

He comes back. She takes the refilled glass.

ANGEL

I was paid to come and say that.

HAROLD

It's—

ANGEL

There was supposed to be dancing and nakedness too.

HAROLD

It's—

She drinks this one down too.

ANGEL

But since you shot me it no longer seems appropriate.

She hands him the glass.

HAROLD

It's not my birthday.

ANGEL
(Reading from the card)
Is this room two-six-zero?

HAROLD

If you say so.

He refills the glass again.

ANGEL

Are you...John?

HAROLD

Who?

She starts to take off her boots.

ANGEL

John. Are you John?

HAROLD

No, I'm Harold.

*He holds out his hand, then ducks as her boot
flies by him.*

                    ANGEL
Stupid fucking switchboard. I hate it when this
happens.

Harold drinks the scotch himself.

                    ANGEL
Unless your friends are playing a joke on you?

                    HAROLD
Not likely. I don't have any.

                    ANGEL
Stupid fucking switchboard.

Furious again, she takes off her other boot.
Harold gets ready to dodge, but she holds on to it
instead of throwing it.

                    ANGEL
They probably gave me the wrong fucking room
number. Again.

                    HAROLD
So that's what Enochian sounds like.

She drops the boot down by the bed.

                    ANGEL
Fuck you, Harold.

                    HAROLD
I'm beginning to think you're not really an Angel.

She makes a rude gesture. He holds out his hand
to her.

HAROLD

Pleased to meet you.

She doesn't take his hand. But she relaxes a bit, propping herself up on the bed.

ANGEL

I could tell from the gunplay. I take it your usual target didn't show.

He's still holding out his hand.

HAROLD

Miss...

She still doesn't shake hands.

ANGEL

Call me Angel.

He pulls back his hand.

HAROLD

I can remember that.

ANGEL

I thought of it in a moment of perspiration.

HAROLD

You mean inspiration.

ANGEL

Not in my line of work.

She removes her halo, sets it on the nightstand next to the gun.

> HAROLD

You're a dancer?

> *She considers him carefully.*

> ANGEL

Yes. Yes, I am.

> HAROLD

What's your real name?

> ANGEL

That's on a need-to-know basis, and you don't.

> *He looks hurt. She relents.*

> ANGEL

Ellie. My name is Ellie.

> HAROLD

Ellie. Nice. Is that short for Ellen?

> ANGEL

No.

> *It's a puzzle.*

> HAROLD

Eleanor?

> ANGEL

No.

> *He has to figure out the answer.*

> HAROLD

Eloise?

She realizes this could go on forever.

ANGEL

Eloa. It's short for Eloa.

He sits on the uttermost edge of the bed.

HAROLD

Eloa. That's beautiful. I never heard that name before.

ANGEL

It's the name of an Angel in some poem. My full name is Eloa Tiriel you don't need to know the rest.

HAROLD

Eloa Tiriel. No wonder you have a nickname.

ANGEL

My Father liked Angels.

Angel sits up, removes her left wing, which is attached with Velcro. Harold winces at the RIPPING sound.

ANGEL

Well, most of them.

She RIPS off the other one.

ANGEL

Here. Put these somewhere safe.

She hands the wings to Harold.

ANGEL

I never wanted to be an Angel. When I grew up, I wanted to be a Dakini.

Harold is enthralled with the wings.

HAROLD

You wanted to be a bathing suit?

ANGEL

Dakini. Not Bikini.

HAROLD

Dakini. Sounds like something with Rum and Pineapple.

ANGEL

It's from Tibetan Buddhism. A Dakini is a Sky Dancer. She's like an Angel only she drinks blood while dancing naked with a string of skulls around her neck.

Harold offers her the wings back.

HAROLD

You can go now.

ANGEL

I'm still a little dizzy.

HAROLD

Must be all that naked dancing.

He attaches the wings to the easel.

HAROLD

Here, I'll open a window.

Angel grabs for his arm as he goes to the window.

ANGEL

Don't! It's too bright out.

He shrugs her off.

HAROLD

It's after midnight.

He opens the blinds. A throbbing red light engulfs the room.

ANGEL

This is Vegas. You can get sunburn at 2 A.M.

He shuts the blinds.

ANGEL

Besides you can't open these windows.

She points to the liquor bottle and snaps her fingers.

ANGEL

They're afraid the losers will jump.

He stumbles half blind to the bottle on the dresser.

ANGEL

What was it? Craps? Blackjack?

He brings her the bottle.

HAROLD

What do you mean?

She takes a long drink. He watches, both alarmed and impressed.

> ANGEL

How much did you lose?

> HAROLD

I don't—

> *She points to the ice bucket and snaps her fingers.*

> ANGEL

You drop the kids college fund?

> HAROLD

No.

> ANGEL

Your retirement?

> HAROLD

No.

> *He brings the ice to her.*

> ANGEL

Then what?

> HAROLD

Nothing!

> *She tugs a pillowcase off a pillow.*

> ANGEL

You were trying to kill yourself.

> *She pours the ice in the pillowcase.*

> ANGEL

On the bed. With the gun. That you shot me with.

She twirls the pillowcase around over her head, twisting it into a ball at the end.

HAROLD

You're wrong.

She holds the icy ball to her head.

ANGEL

So I assumed you lost big.

He doesn't answer. She points to the noose.

ANGEL

Look. It was either that or you were practicing for Wild Bill's All Nude Rodeo down the street.

HAROLD

I said you're wrong.

ANGEL

Eight shows a day. Good money.

Harold again sinks down on the bed, facing away from her.

HAROLD

It's none of your business.

ANGEL

You made it my business when you shot me.

HAROLD

I didn't shoot you. I shot at you.

ANGEL

I'm so relieved. But why all this?

STEPHEN EVANS

She swats at the noose.

ANGEL

Rope? Gun? Pills? How dead can you get?

*He climbs up on the bed and starts taking down
the noose.*

HAROLD

I just wanted to be certain.

ANGEL

Certain? Of what?

HAROLD

Certain that I died.

ANGEL

I can see in your case it might be hard to tell.

Harold unties the noose and climbs down.

HAROLD

What do you mean?

ANGEL

Just that it's customary to live first.

HAROLD

I lived. Live. Am living.

ANGEL

You seem tenseless.

HAROLD

I am completely tense. Look. Okay, so I tried to kill myself. What are you going to do? Tell me everything's okay? Just talk it through and everything will be wonderful?

She considers, shrugs: her signature response to events.

ANGEL

Doesn't sound like me.

He puts the noose away.

HAROLD

You don't know anything about me.

ANGEL

When you carry firearms, you're not exactly a conversation magnet.

He goes to the door and opens it. Casino bells blast in.

HAROLD

Look. You seem like you're okay. I'm sorry if I scared you. If you need money, there's some in my wallet. Please take it and go.

She gets up and goes to the wallet. She looks in and fans out some bills.

ANGEL

Well, I guess you didn't lose everything.

Harold lets the door shut.

HAROLD

I've lost everything. And I'm not even a gambler.

She puts the bills back in the wallet.

ANGEL

Maybe you lost everything because you're not a gambler.

She looks at his credit cards.

ANGEL

If you're not here to gamble, why are you here?

HAROLD

I'm here for a conference.

ANGEL

Ah, the International Society of Suicides. I hear membership is declining.

She unfolds the clear plastic insert. No pictures.

HAROLD

No, cosmology.

ANGEL

The study of makeup.

HAROLD

Not cosmetology. Cosmology.

ANGEL

Big subject.

HAROLD

There are more things in heaven and earth, Horatio, than are dreamt of in your philosophy.

She drops the wallet back on the dresser.

ANGEL

Don't call me Horatio. Well, maybe the first part.

Harold goes the door and opens it. Casino bells blast in.

HAROLD

Look, I'm kind of busy here. I'd really like you to leave.

Angel goes to the board covered with equations.

ANGEL

Are these your equations?

He lets the door swing shut. It closes tight this time too.

HAROLD

Please don't touch that. That's my suicide note.

She picks up the marker and puts little bells at the corner of the board.

HAROLD

Why did you do that?

ANGEL

It's Christmas.

HAROLD

Those equations are standard derivations of the theorem of Nonlocality. Also known as Bell's Theorem. Have you ever heard of Bell's Theorem?

> ANGEL

No.

> HAROLD

Would you like me to explain?

> ANGEL

No.

Harold settles into his teaching voice and manner.

> HAROLD

Bell's Theorem asserts—

> ANGEL

No means no.

> HAROLD

That there is some unknowable connection between elementary particles—

> ANGEL

Just Say No.

> HAROLD

Where when something happens to one of the particles—

> ANGEL

There's no business like show business?

> HAROLD

The other changes immediately, no matter how far apart they are.

Angel picks up her wings from the easel.

ANGEL

Did you ever see that movie where they say that every time a bell rings, an Angel gets her wings?

HAROLD

It's called Entanglement. Though Einstein referred to it as spooky action at a distance.

ANGEL

I think the wingmaker must have been really pissed off when they invented slot machines.

Harold examines his equations and chuckles again.

HAROLD

It was a little inside joke for my colleagues. Suicide. Nonlocality. Bells. Seek not to know...

Angel puts the wings back.

HAROLD

Forget it.

ANGEL

SAAAD.

HAROLD

Not really.

ANGEL

That's what it spells. Spooky Action At A Distance.

She writes in the air.

ANGEL

S-A-A-A-D. SAAAD.

> HAROLD

Do you always think in acronyms?

> ANGEL

Just something my mind does automatically.

She writes in the air again.

JSMMDA.

> HAROLD

Now that's SAAAD.

> ANGEL

Sometimes I think entirely in acronyms. SITEIA.
Saves time.

> HAROLD

ST. I get the picture.

> ANGEL

Spooky action at a distance. That describes every
boyfriend I ever had.

He refuses to be distracted.

> HAROLD

Look. I'm trying to do something important here.

*He goes the door and opens it. Casino bells blast
in.*

> HAROLD

Please leave.

> ANGEL

So I imagine you've thought this through.

He slams the door shut in frustration.

HAROLD

Of course I've thought it through.

She goes to the dresser, plays with the coins.

ANGEL

Thought it through completely, like the intelligent man you are. If you don't mind my using that term.

HAROLD

Yes. Completely. Completely through. Why?

She notices the CD player, is a little surprised, fingers the buttons.

ANGEL

I was just wondering what you wish to come back as?

HAROLD

What do you mean?

ANGEL

You know. Reincarnation.

HAROLD

There's no such thing as reincarnation.

She takes out the CD.

ANGEL

Are you sure?

HAROLD

There's no convincing scientific evidence supporting it.

She doesn't recognize it, puts it back.

ANGEL

Are you 'certain'?

ANGEL	HAROLD
I think you're getting your epistemology confused with your ontology. I mean positivism is empirically useful, but it is by definition as self-limiting as, say, phenomenology.	Of course I'm not certain. The point is. The point is. Certainty is, in physics, in anything. The point is, which they don't see, is that I'm here because, because, because I don't know why I'm here.

Pause.

ANGEL	HAROLD
What?	What?

Pause.

ANGEL	HAROLD
It is the height of arrogance to say that only what I can see and measure can be real, especially for creatures who haven't been around that long on the universal scale.	We are an unintended complexity, an undesired byproduct floating over an essential reality that not only doesn't care, but is fundamentally unaware, that we even exist.

Pause.

ANGEL   HAROLD

What?   What?

He sighs. Now he goes for the scotch.

HAROLD

You can't have reincarnation without something to
reincarnate. I see no evidence that people have souls.
To me, the evidence seems quite to the contrary.

ANGEL

Oh I can prove you have a soul.

She begins to stretch.

HAROLD

You can prove it? Logically?

More stretching.

ANGEL

A completely logical proof.

HAROLD

That I would like to hear.

ANGEL

Okay.

She jumps onto the bed.

ANGEL

Fuck me.

Harold turns away.

> HAROLD

I...uh...uh...no. Thank you.

Angel sits up in Lotus position.

> ANGEL

See? There you go. You have a soul.

> HAROLD

Because I wouldn't...

> ANGEL

No. Because you have free will.

He glances back.

> HAROLD

Oh...I...uh...well?

She writhes sensuously on the bed.

> ANGEL

And you can't have free will without a soul.

His curiosity overcomes his embarrassment.

> HAROLD

How do you figure?

> ANGEL

Simple. Free will can't exist in a strictly material process.

Angel again moves into Lotus position.

ANGEL

Look, logically, any physical process has to be either random or non-random, right?

HAROLD

One or the other, I guess. Sure.

She evolves into another yoga position, more erotic.

ANGEL

If your decision process is random, then it's not free will because it's not will at all. There's no intent. It's random.

HAROLD

Wait.

She twists into a third yoga position.

ANGEL

Now if your decision process is not random.

Then leaps into a cartwheel.

ANGEL

Then each decision point is equivalent to a determinative physical state, and the decision process is simply a computation of these various physical states using some biochemically inspired algorithm.

Into a handstand.

> ANGEL

No matter how complex the algorithm, it's still not free will because each state is physically pre-determined.

> HAROLD

Wow.

She walks up to him on her hands.

> ANGEL

Free will is really free. And to be really free, it must have a non-physical source.

She flips to an upright position.

> ANGEL

Hence the soul.

She falls backward onto the bed.

> ANGEL

Hence, reincarnation. Hence—

She transforms again into the Lotus position.

> ANGEL

What do you wish to come back as?

Harold backs away.

> HAROLD

You know, I bet I do have free will. My decision-making process could never have evolved naturally. I'd be extinct by now.

Moving her hands like an Indian dancer.

ANGEL

Stop avoiding the issue.

Harold brightens.

HAROLD

I know. I'll come back as God.

ANGEL

Bad choice.

HAROLD

Why?

ANGEL

You'd have only yourself to blame.

HAROLD

True. Okay. You tell me. What do you see me coming back as?

She considers him closely for a moment, intensely enough to make Harold self-conscious.

ANGEL

A train whistle.

HAROLD

Why?

ANGEL

Because no matter where you are you're always leaving.

Harold then considers her. She is completely comfortable, which makes him uncomfortable.

HAROLD

Do you know what I see you as? A cloud.

She is charmed by his answer.

ANGEL

Really? That's sweet!

HAROLD

Because no matter where you are, you're always raining on something!

ANGEL

Oh.

HAROLD

I'm trying to commit suicide here and I want to feel good about it.

ANGEL

Well, I'm sorry.

She is. He relents.

HAROLD

It's not your fault. You're just optimistic.

ANGEL

I'm just as depressed as you are.

HAROLD

You are not.

ANGEL

I am too.

HAROLD

You're practically cheerful. You come in here "la la la, I'm an Angel". You virtually floated in here.

ANGEL

I virtually floated in here because I fainted after you shot me.

HAROLD

That is just...just...Just. But the point is I'm suicidal and you're leaving.

He goes to the door and opens it.

Casino bells blast in.

ANGEL

I'm not leaving.

HAROLD

Yes you are.

ANGEL

What are you going to do? Shoot me again?

He lets the door close.

HAROLD

No. No. Look. Please. This is very private. I can't kill myself with an audience.

ANGEL

Why?

HAROLD

It would be rude.

> ANGEL

Rude?

> HAROLD

Rude. It would be rude.

Angel crosses to the gun.

> ANGEL

Okay. Okay. I'll leave.

She picks up the gun.

> HAROLD

Thank you.

She moves to the door, squeezes between the door and Harold.

> ANGEL

With you.

They are very close. This time Harold doesn't back off. But her proximity is very disconcerting.

> HAROLD

Look. I appreciate what you're trying to do. But it won't work. There's nothing you can do to stop me.

> ANGEL

I'm not trying to stop you.

> HAROLD

You're a very sweet person to try and—what?

> ANGEL

I'm not trying to stop you.

HAROLD

You're not?

She points the gun at her head.

ANGEL

I'll leave with you.

*Harold is puzzled at first, then understands—
she's proposing a double suicide.*

HAROLD

No.

ANGEL

Yes.

HAROLD

You mean?

ANGEL

Yes.

HAROLD

No!

ANGEL

Yes!

*She stops him from speaking by putting the gun
to his lips.*

ANGEL

Don't argue. It's rude.

*Now he moves away, trying to get his mind
around the concept.*

HAROLD

Why?

Angel's eyes flash with anger.

ANGEL

What? You think I can give you a two-minute monologue that will explain my life to you, that will explain my pain to you, the losses I have suffered from which I will never recover, from which no one ever recovers?

HAROLD

I'm sorry.

ANGEL

You can't derive this from the sum of my histories.

Harold is taken aback by the phrase.

HAROLD

That's quantum physics.

ANGEL

What?

HAROLD

Sum of my histories. That's what you do to a particle. To calculate the probability of an event, you sum up the possible histories of the—

She holds up the gun.

ANGEL

Make up your mind. Do you want to talk or do you want to...not talk.

HAROLD

What? No. You are free to do what you want on your own, but if you want to do this with me, I need to know why.

She looks in the mirror.

ANGEL

How's this: the soul is like a jukebox. There are lots of songs inside. If you don't like the current song, push the button and make your next selection.

HAROLD

Won't this give you bad Karma or something?

She laughs.

ANGEL

Oh yeah, I'm just really racking up the good Karma in this life.

HAROLD

But you're not like me. You're smart. You're beautiful.

ANGEL

You're sweet, Harold. Naïve but sweet. In this life, I'll always be...Horatio.

HAROLD

You're wrong.

ANGEL

This is my chance.

HAROLD

Chance for what?

She pulls his arm around her. The hand with the gun is at her breast.

ANGEL

To not die alone.

He nods. This he understands.

HAROLD

Entanglement.

ANGEL

Exactly.

HAROLD

Okay.

Angel claps her hands. The decision made, she is all business.

ANGEL

So. How do we do it?

HAROLD

Do it?

ANGEL

Should we stab each other?

Harold winces.

HAROLD

Won't that hurt?

ANGEL

Think how effective it will be.

HAROLD

I don't have any knives.

ANGEL

Swords? Bayonets? Scissors?

HAROLD

Sorry.

ANGEL

I thought all men carried something sharp.

HAROLD

I used to carry a fountain pen. But it jammed.

ANGEL

A common problem in men your age.

She takes the gun.

ANGEL

Well then, you could shoot me—you have some experience at that—then shoot yourself.

HAROLD

That won't work.

ANGEL

Why not?

Harold takes the gun and removes the clip. It's empty.

HAROLD

There was only one bullet in the gun.

ANGEL

Who buys only one bullet?

She examines the clip.

HAROLD

I didn't want anyone else to get hurt by accident.

She gives it back.

ANGEL

That was very polite of you, considering you'd be dead.

He drops the empty clip and gun on the dresser.

HAROLD

Anyway, I was sort of hoping to be asleep when I killed myself.

ANGEL

Pills! That will work.

He glances down.

HAROLD

They were in my hand. Now they're all over the floor.

She goes to her purse, reaches in, pulls out a bottle of pills.

ANGEL

Here. We can use these.

HAROLD

Oh. What are they?

ANGEL

Trust me. They'll do the job.

She opens the childproof cap.

ANGEL

The guy who sold them to me promised. And he's killed enough people to know.

HAROLD

What are you doing with them?

She gives him a look: isn't it obvious?

HAROLD

Oh. I see. But there are two of us now.

ANGEL

Enough to kill a chorus line, that's what he said. Trust me on this.

Harold nods. They head for opposite sides of the bed.

HAROLD

You say "trust me" a lot.

ANGEL

If you can't trust an Angel, who can you trust?

He can't argue with that.

HAROLD

Well, let's do it.

She starts to take off her costume.

HAROLD

What are you doing?

She stops.

ANGEL

I'm getting ready to do it.

HAROLD

Do what exactly?

ANGEL

I'm getting undressed.

HAROLD

I see that. Why?

ANGEL

It's customary.

HAROLD

What is?

ANGEL

When you commit suicide, you have to be naked.

She crawls over the bed to his side.

ANGEL

It's the rule.

HAROLD

No one ever told me that.

She helps him off with his jacket.

ANGEL

Don't you remember that movie, A Star is Born?

She unhooks his cummerbund.

ANGEL

At the end, when James Mason walks down to the ocean, he drops his robe.

HAROLD

You mean?

ANGEL

Buck.

She takes off his bow tie.

HAROLD

But he was English?

ANGEL

That's why he followed the rule.

HAROLD

Why, though?

She slides down his suspenders.

ANGEL

I don't know.

She unbuttons his shirt.

ANGEL

Maybe that way, the people who find you can at least think you had some fun first.

HAROLD

Oh. I always thought you dressed up for suicide.

She undoes the cufflinks.

ANGEL

Oh no. Black tie is definitely wrong. Nudity is proper
for double suicide.

She pulls off his shirt.

HAROLD

That has no basis in rational thought.

ANGEL

De gustibus non disputandem est.

HAROLD

Excuse me?

ANGEL

Don't they teach Latin anymore? I said there is no
disputing taste.

She rests her hands lightly on his chest.

ANGEL

Unless of course you're a televAngelist.

HAROLD

Wait. Let me turn out the light.

Angel shrugs and gets in bed.

ANGEL

Suit yourself.

*He turns out the light. The pulsing red neon glare
filters through the curtains, alternately
illuminating the room dimly and leaving it dark.*

HAROLD

I have the pills. Here are yours.

He blindly tries to find her hand, and finds other things instead.

HAROLD

Oh, sorry! I didn't mean...I mean...

ANGEL

It's okay.

HAROLD

I'm a little nervous.

ANGEL

Me too.

HAROLD

It's my first suicide.

ANGEL

Mine too.

Harold takes charge.

HAROLD

Okay. We swallow on three.

ANGEL

Don't worry. I'm a professional.

HAROLD

One.

ANGEL

One.

                    HAROLD
Two.

                    ANGEL
Two.

                    HAROLD
Three.

                    ANGEL
Three.

   Neither moves.

                    HAROLD
Did you?

                    ANGEL
No.

                    HAROLD
Are you afraid?

                    ANGEL
Yes.

                    HAROLD
Me too.

   He sighs. Then she sighs.

                    HAROLD
You know what I'm afraid of most? That it won't be
the end. That my mind will just go on and on and on
with nothing to stop it, forever.

                    ANGEL
Like TelevAngelists.

HAROLD

Televangelists.

ANGEL

TelevAngelists.

HAROLD

If you say so.

Angel moves closer to him.

ANGEL

In the books, they say admit what you fear.

HAROLD

I just did.

ANGEL

I mean embrace it.

Angel moves next to him. She puts her hand to his cheek, turns his head toward her.

ANGEL

I'll put them in your mouth and you put them in mine.

HAROLD

That's assisted suicide.

ANGEL

So they can put us in jail afterwards.

HAROLD

Oh right. Okay, it's a deal.

ANGEL

Here, take a drink first.

She gives him a drink from the bottle of scotch.

ANGEL

Ready? On three. One. Two. Three.

They swallow.

HAROLD

Did you?

ANGEL

Yes.

HAROLD

Me too.

Angel sits on the bed, back against the headboard. Harold joins her. There is a long pause.

HAROLD

Why couldn't this have happened last night?

ANGEL

What?

HAROLD

Nothing.

She settles in next to him.

ANGEL

You have a nice mouth.

HAROLD

So do you. You have nice eyes.

ANGEL

You can't see my eyes.

HAROLD

I know. I just...you sound like you have nice eyes.

ANGEL

Would you hold me, Harold?

HAROLD

Oh God yes.

ANGEL

Are you feeling sleepy yet?

HAROLD

I don't feel anything. Honest.

ANGEL

I'm not sleepy yet either.

She snuggles into him.

ANGEL

Closer.

HAROLD

Yes, it's closer.

ANGEL

Hold me closer.

He does.

HAROLD

Like that?

ANGEL

Just.

HAROLD

So.

Harold laughs nervously.

HAROLD

There's something I've always wanted to know. How many Angels can dance on the head of a pin?

She rolls on top of him.

ANGEL

Depends on the size of the pin.

She kisses him.

Blackout.

End of Act I.

Act II Scene 1

Setting: The Twilight Zone

At Rise: A door floats in empty space against a backdrop of stars. Harold is standing in front of the door.

The door swings open. Angel is framed in a blinding blinking red light.

HAROLD

Who are you?

ANGEL

I'm the Angel of Death.

Harold breaks out in laughter.

ANGEL

What?

Blackout.

STEPHEN EVANS

Act II Scene 2

Setting: The Twilight Zone

At Rise: A door floats in empty space against a
                  backdrop of stars.

*Harold speaks using a microphone from the back
of the theater, as in the musical A Chorus Line.*

HAROLD

Number...260?

*A reddish spotlight flares. Angel reluctantly
walks through the door into the spotlight. She
peers beyond the stage.*

ANGEL

That's me.

HAROLD

What's your name?

ANGEL

Angel.

HAROLD

I didn't ask what part you were auditioning for. I
asked your name.

ANGEL

Angel. That is my name. My stage name.

> *She starts looking around for something.*

HAROLD

I see. Okay, what part are you auditioning for?

ANGEL

Angel.

HAROLD

How convenient.

ANGEL

I thought of it—

HAROLD

I know. What number are you going to do?

> *A CD player appears in another spot.*

ANGEL

I'm not sure I have the right music.

HAROLD

Look Miss...Angel, we don't have forever. Well, actually, we do, but...

ANGEL

I understand. Okay.

> *She starts the CD player, then runs into place center stage. The music of Thus Spake Zarathustra booms out, the same segment Harold was playing earlier.*

Angel performs her graceful and erotic Angel Dancer. Before she's finished, Harold interrupts her.

HAROLD

Thank you.

She switches off the music.

HAROLD

We'll call you.

Angel nods. She knows what that means. She's almost out the door when:

HAROLD

Honestly, I'm not sure you're Angel material.

ANGEL

But that's all I want to be.

HAROLD

Look, I realize that these are very subjective judgments, but I am the Director.

She heads downstage and speaks into the darkness.

ANGEL

You may be the Director but you aren't God.

HAROLD

Well...okay, look, I'm a merciful guy. Tell me something: what is it that you want to do most?

Angel starts to speak. He cuts her off.

HAROLD

Don't say be an Angel. Don't tell me what you want to be. What do you want to do?

ANGEL

I want to...discover a cure for cancer.

HAROLD

I see. Anything else?

ANGEL

I want to...end world hunger.

HAROLD

(bored)
I see. Anything else?

She's desperate.

ANGEL

I want to dance!

HAROLD

I see.

ANGEL

It's what I do.

HAROLD

I see.

ANGEL

It's what I do!

HAROLD

I see.

ANGEL

Anything else?

HAROLD

(Muttering to himself)
I have enough damned Angels as it is.

ANGEL

I see.

Harold sighs, LOUDLY, a Dolby rumble that shakes the theater.

HAROLD

Tell the costumer to redo those wings. I don't want them drooping on stage. Got it?

ANGEL

Yes, sir. Thank you, sir.

HAROLD

Now get out of here.

ANGEL

You won't regret it.

HAROLD

I never do.

Blackout.

STEPHEN EVANS

Act II Scene 3

Setting: The Twilight Zone

At Rise: A door floats in empty space against a
                  backdrop of stars. Harold is standing in
                  front of the door.

*The door swings open. Angel is framed in a
blinding blinking red light.*

HAROLD

Who are you?

Harold breaks out in laughter.

ANGEL

What?

Blackout.

STEPHEN EVANS

ACT II Scene 4

Setting: The Twilight Zone

At Rise: A door floats in empty space against a
                   backdrop of stars. Harold and Angel
                   are standing in front of the door.

Harold looks around.

HAROLD

Where am I?

ANGEL

You're dying.

*He points at her, nervous as Scrooge on
Christmas eve.*

HAROLD

Who are you?

ANGEL

I'm the Angel of near-death.

Harold drops the nervous act and corrects her.

HAROLD

Don't you mean the Angel of death?

ANGEL

I'm working my way up.

Back to Scrooge, quaking.

HAROLD

Why are you here?

ANGEL

It's a job.

HAROLD

No. I mean. Why Are You Here?

Angel gestures like a model on a game show.

ANGEL

(bored)
I'm here to show you what life would be like if you had never lived.

Harold is delighted. He was in the wrong movie.

HAROLD

Oh. I got it. Like the movie. Go ahead.

He looks around expectantly, which makes her look around too. He gestures: Well?

ANGEL

This is it.

HAROLD

What do you mean this is it? I don't see anything.

ANGEL

Of course you don't see anything. You're dead.

He looks around again.

HAROLD

But this is boring.

ANGEL

You're telling me. I can't wait to get promoted.

HAROLD

No. I mean not living is boring. Really boring.

ANGEL

Yeah. Boy, did you make a mistake.

HAROLD

It's not funny.

She holds up a deck of cards.

ANGEL

I brought a deck of cards.

She starts shuffling.

HAROLD

Wait! This isn't right. You're supposed to show me all the terrible things that would have happened if I never lived.

ANGEL

Oh yeah. I always forget that part.

She peers off toward the audience.

ANGEL

Nope. Everything is fine.

HAROLD

What do you mean everything is fine? Check again.

ANGEL

Okay.

She peers off toward the audience again. She starts to laugh.

ANGEL

Oh yeah, they're having fun. Party time!!!

HAROLD

What?

ANGEL

Your sister got your room. She loved that.

HAROLD

Wait, what about my brother? I saved him from drowning.

ANGEL

Well, yes, but you were the one who wanted to go swimming in the first place. He went to a baseball game instead. Met a cheerleader.

HAROLD

So it didn't matter?

ANGEL

Well, I mean come on. You are just a bit of unintended complexity, you know that.

She starts to deal the cards.

Blackout.

Act II Scene 5

Setting: The Twilight Zone

At Rise: A door floats in empty space against a
                  backdrop of stars. Harold is standing in
                  front of the door.

*Playwright's Note: the letters in the following
lines are each pronounced individually, as in an
acronym (or Initialism, to be precise)/*

HAROLD

W A Y.

ANGEL

I A T A O D.

HAROLD

D B N P, T S H C T

M A D, F T A N S;

F T W T T T D O,

D N, P D, N Y C T K M.

F R A S, W B T P B,

M P; T F T M M M F,

A S O B M W T D G,

STEPHEN EVANS

R O T B, A S D.

T A S T F, C, K, A D M,

A D W P, W, A S D;

A P O C C M U S A W

A B T T S; W S T T?

O S S P, W W E,

A D S B N M; D, T S D.

ANGEL

O K.

Blackout.

Act II Scene 6

Setting: The Twilight Zone

At Rise: A door floats in empty space against a backdrop of stars. The door has shrunk to the size of a podium and Harold stands behind it. There is a huge book on the podium, thousands and thousands of pages long. To the side, a blank white board on an easel, also elongated out of shape.

HAROLD

It's a bit dark in here.

ANGEL

Let there be light.

Harold is hit by a brilliant blue spotlight. Angel is sitting in the front row of the audience.

HAROLD

Someone's been reading ahead.

Harold clears his throat, drinks some water.

HAROLD

Welcome to Divinity School.

There's a general voiceover muttering from the invisible 'audience'.

HAROLD

I know. Someone of you are wondering 'Why?'

The muttering gets louder.

HAROLD

I'm all powerful. I'm omniscient. Why do I have to attend a conference on how to be a god?"

Harold holds out his hands, calming.

HAROLD

Every god thinks he's ready to direct a universe. But what we will present to you at this conference will save you eons of bad reviews. So let's get started.

He claps his hands. Thunder sounds.

HAROLD

The first thing I want to go over is the curriculum vitae. If you'll turn your workbooks to page six times ten to the minus 15.

He turns the pages in the enormous book, back and back and back to the first page.

HAROLD

In the beginning will be the word. Please do not repeat the word to others. If you do, we have to pick another word and it means reprinting a lot of stationery.

He turns a page, then puts on reading glasses.

HAROLD

Day One: Divide light from darkness. Call the light Day and the dark Night. Apply quality control techniques and see that it is good.

Another page.

HAROLD

Day Two: Divide the waters from the waters. Make the Earth and seas. Invest in real estate in Malibu. See that it is Oceanfront.

Another page.

HAROLD

Day Three: Let the earth bring forth grass. Talk about lawn care.

Another page.

HAROLD

Day Four: Set lights in the firmament of heaven. Emphasize the importance of proper lighting.

Another page.

HAROLD

Day Five: Bring forth living creatures. Remind me to mention snakes.

Another page.

HAROLD

Day Six: Create male and female. Be fruitful and multiply. By the way, this is not a section about mathematics.

And finally.

HAROLD

Day Seven: Take a break.

He takes off his reading glasses.

HAROLD

Let's please try and keep the break to no more than 13.8 billion years.

He closes the book with an enormous crash that resounds throughout the known universe.

HAROLD

But before we move on to Day One, I want to throw out a question for you: Why? Why do you want to direct a universe.

Some of the answers I've heard before are:

a) I'm bored.

b) It's lonely at the top.

c) All the other gods have one.

What do you think about those answers?

Angel makes a rude noise.

HAROLD

Exactly. None of those answers are very satisfying, are they? So you have two choices. You can spend ages in analysis trying to understand your inner Godot. Or you can think in these terms: what do you want your universe to do?

He begins to pace across the stage.

HAROLD

Most universes do something; they are active, not static. Static universes are really only good for Christmas presents. They look great in one of those little crystal balls where you shake them up and watch the galaxies float around.

He stops in front of the white board and picks up a marker.

HAROLD

But for the long run, and, trust me, eternity is a long run, you need an active universe. By definition, an active universe has a Purpose.

He writes PURPOSE on the white board.

HAROLD

So the first question you have to answer as a director is what is the purpose of the universe?

He goes back to the podium, consults his notes.

HAROLD

Here's a hint. Pick an action verb. Something simple. I know, you all think you're ready for parallel universes of infinite number. But frankly, that just takes too long to grade. So, something simple. To Worship. To Love. To...

ANGEL

Dance?

He's pleased.

> HAROLD

Dance!

> *He writes DANCE on the board.*

> HAROLD

Okay, that's good. So. Dancing is your purpose. How would you set up the universe?

> *No answer.*

> HAROLD

What do you need?

> ANGEL

Space.

> HAROLD

Exactly. If you want dancing, you need.

> *He writes SPACE on the board.*

> HAROLD

And lots of it. You don't want your dancers cramped into a tiny stage. And not just space, you need mostly...

> ANGEL

Empty space?

> HAROLD

Exactly.

> *He writes EMPTY before space on the board.*

HAROLD

You don't want your dancers tripping over things
either. One misplaced black hole can do a lot of
damage, trust me.

*He points to the cluttered event horizon behind
him.*

HAROLD

So you want your space uncluttered for the most part.
Okay, you have empty space. What else do you need?
Anyone? Any duality? Any trinity?

ANGEL

Time.

HAROLD

Exactly. To dance, you need motion. And for motion
you need.

He writes TIME on the board after space.

HAROLD

Time is one of the hardest concepts for eternal beings
to comprehend.

He draws a bell on its side.

HAROLD

Look at this illustration. This is what time looks like to
us: motion through multiple dimensions. Nothing is
lost. Time is growth.

He draws perpendicular lines through the bell.

> HAROLD

Now observe.

He points.

> HAROLD

These lines are what motion looks like from within space-time. You can see that there is a sense of one thing replacing another at each point on the cone. Got it? Well make some time and work on it.

Okay, we have space. We have time. What else do we need?

> ANGEL

Dancers.

> HAROLD

Makes sense, right? Can't have dancing without—.

He writes DANCERS on the board.

> HAROLD

So what kind of dancers do we want?

> ANGEL

Beautiful. Flowing. Light.

> HAROLD

Beautiful flowing light.

He writes LIGHT on the board.

> HAROLD

We want to fill our universe with—

ANGEL

Beautiful flowing light, dancing, spinning, waving, filling the fabric of the empty universe with rapturous, ecstatic motion.

HAROLD

There's your mission statement.

He puts down the marker.

HAROLD

Now as a director, eventually you are going to want to just sit back and watch, not take an active eon to eon part in the dance, but just enjoy it as it unfolds before you. Once you get to this point, you will need to add...

ANGEL

Dance captains.

HAROLD

Exactly. Dance captains. These dance captains, also known as,

He writes Angels on the board.

HAROLD

Will keep the action moving according to your divine orders.

So. That's our project. Our universe. Dance-Empty-Space-Time-Light-Angels. So how do we start?

There is muttering but no answer.

HAROLD

All you have to do is ring a bell. Every time a bell rings, a universe is born. This is known as Bell's Theorem.

He laughs.

HAROLD

Now of course, it's not quite that simple, as you might expect. You have to ring the bell with just the right tonality to produce the appropriate cosmological constants. Yes, question?

A red spotlight hits Angel, who is sitting in the audience.

ANGEL

As a director, do you show or tell? In other words, do you get up on stage and show the dancers what to do, or do you stand outside the dance and direct.

Harold sits on the edge of the stage and talks to her.

HAROLD

Excellent question. My preference is to stand outside. Your dancers learn more. Plus you keep your perspective.

Angel raises her hand. He calls on her.

ANGEL

So how do you teach?

HAROLD

For 99.9999999% of creation, you won't need to. But for the few, the special, the conscious, you need to work a little harder.

ANGEL

How do you do that?

HAROLD

Several ways. You can issue—

He goes back to the podium, puts his glasses back on.

HAROLD

Commandments.

He takes off his glasses.

HAROLD

Commandments can be very effective. But be careful how many you issue. Ten is too many. Nobody can remember ten commandments. I say, pick your top three. Personally, I prefer: Love your God, Dance with Beauty, and Smile at the Audience. Short, clear, and to the point. Which reminds me.

He steps out from behind the podium.

HAROLD

I know some of you think that writing your commandments in stone is the way to go. But, trust me, stone is just too bulky. I have found more discarded commandments at yard sales than I'd care to mention.

Angel is taking careful notes.

ANGEL

What if commandments don't work?

HAROLD

Well, then you can try writing a sacred text. If you don't have time to write it yourself, you can use a ghost writer.

He sits at the edge of the stage again.

HAROLD

But here's a tip: If the ghost writer says he wants to write in dialogue, confine him immediately to perdition. Dialogue is the refuge of the charlatan.

ANGEL

What if you are under a time crunch? You know, the birth of a messiah or the end of a millennium?

HAROLD

Then you can split the job into parts. However, this can be a real management headache. You know, what if Matthew isn't speaking to Mark, and so forth. Writers are like that.

ANGEL

What if the book isn't enough?

HAROLD

Then pick a prophet. I recommend staying away from burning bushes except in major media markets where you can get a lot of TV coverage. Otherwise they're just bad for the environment. My advice is to pick a talk show host. They're well dressed, and they'll do pretty much anything for ratings.

Harold stands and walks the stage again.

HAROLD

You can even have your talk show host promote your sacred text. This is known in the trade as a televAngelist. Be warned: they will take a high percentage of the profits. But as the saying goes, it takes a profit to make a prophet.

ANGEL

And if that doesn't work?

HAROLD

There's one more thing you can try: it is called a—

He writes MIRACLE on the board.

HAROLD

This is also known in the trade as Spooky Action at a Distance.

He writes: S A A A D.

ANGEL

How do you create a miracle?

HAROLD

All it takes is a pair of dice.

He picks a pair of dice out of the quantum void.

ANGEL

Any final suggestions?

HAROLD

Just this: don't lose your sense of humor. Trust me, six days out of seven you'll wish you could just hang out a sign that says God is dead, back on Monday. But that seventh day can be paradise.

So.

Let there be Dark.

Blackout.

Act II Scene 7

Setting: The Twilight Zone

At Rise: The hotel room floats in empty space
against a backdrop of stars. Harold is
standing in front of the door.

The door swings open. Angel is framed in a
blinking red light.

HAROLD

Who are you?

ANGEL

The possibility - to pass Without a Moment's Bell -
Into Conjecture's presence - Is like a Face of Steel -
That suddenly looks into ours With a metallic grin -
The Cordiality of Death - Who drills her Welcome in
-

Harold holds the door open and she enters. He
closes the door and moves toward the window.

Angel opens the blinds. The bright red light is
blinking, blinding, on and off.

Harold tries to "go into the light" when the light
is on, and steps back when its off.

He does this numerous times.

Angel closes the blinds, goes to him, leads him back to bed.

Blackout.

End of Act II.

Act III Scene 1

Setting: The hotel room.

At Rise: The flashing red light is still flashing, alternately illuminating the room dimly and leaving it dark. Harold and Angel are in bed.

Harold sits up in bed, startled.

HAROLD
Wait. Where? Wow.

He gets out of bed. He's not wearing his pants.

HAROLD
Heaven looks a lot like Vegas.

He sees Angel.

HAROLD
Oh my God. I killed her again!

He climbs over her, again starts CPR. As he is giving her mouth-to-mouth resuscitation, her eyes open.

ANGEL
Huh huh huh huhhuh. (This still costs extra).

Harold sits up in shock.

> ANGEL

This still costs extra.

> HAROLD

You're alive.

He kisses her.

> ANGEL

Do you have like a sleeping beauty fetish?

He tries to pull her out of bed.

> HAROLD

Here, get up. We have to walk you around.

> ANGEL

Yeah, that's just what I want to do.

> HAROLD

But what if...

She pushes him away.

> ANGEL

I'm okay. Are you okay?

> HAROLD

I'm okay. I'm okay. I can't be okay. But I'm okay.

> ANGEL

You're okay.

She sits up. She is wearing Harold's shirt. He notices that he is not wearing pants and pulls them on.

HAROLD

What time is it?

He goes to the curtains.

ANGEL

Don't!

He opens the curtains and is again engulfed in blinking red.

ANGEL

This is Vegas. If the sun is blinking, it's night.

He closes the curtains.

HAROLD

Why aren't we dead?

ANGEL

(*sarcastic*)
It's a miracle.

HAROLD

Maybe it was the...you know.

ANGEL

What?

HAROLD

You know...

ANGEL

Give me a hint.

He gestures with his middle finger.

ANGEL

Yeah well fuck you too. Oh, the sex? You think it was the sex? I've raised a lot of things but never the dead.

HAROLD

Maybe the hormones interacted with the chemical structure of the pills, changing them into stimulants.

He sits on the bed next to her.

HAROLD

I did seem stimulated.

ANGEL

And you think it was the pills? I beg your pardon.

HAROLD

There has to be a logical explanation.

She gets out of bed, looking around for something.

ANGEL

I told you, it was a miracle.

HAROLD

Don't be ridiculous.

ANGEL

Obviously I am an Angel and God sent me here to spare your life.

Harold sums the histories.

HAROLD

Right. Right? Right!

ANGEL

What?

She finds a boot and sits to put it on.

HAROLD

It fits.

ANGEL

It should.

HAROLD

The hypothesis explains the observed behavior.

ANGEL

What's to explain. It's a boot. I'm putting it on.

HAROLD

But is it verifiable?

ANGEL

It looks like a boot to me.

HAROLD

We need a test.

ANGEL

I could kick you with it.

HAROLD

No. You're an Angel. It's a miracle.

ANGEL

I should kick you with it.

She puts the boot on.

HAROLD

What?

ANGEL

Other than the costume, what could possibly lead you to think of me as Angelic?

She continues the search.

HAROLD

You performed a miracle. That's pretty convincing evidence.

ANGEL

I performed several things. They were spectacular, but not miraculous.

Harold evaluates the operant possibilities.

HAROLD

We can't automatically assume that you would know you were an Angel.

She finds part of her costume and puts it on. She keeps looking.

ANGEL

What, I'm an unconscious Angel?

He traces her initial movements back to the door.

HAROLD

You fell.

ANGEL

Oh, now I'm a fallen Angel.

HAROLD

You fell and you hit your head so you have Angel amnesia. Angelnesia.

ANGEL

I'd like to forget you.

HAROLD

If you're not an Angel, how did you know about punctuated equilibrium?

He starts following her around as she searches.

ANGEL

Ballet class?

HAROLD

And summing histories. And Bell's theorem. They don't teach those at ballet class.

ANGEL

When was the last time you took a ballet class?

HAROLD

There's more to you than meets the eye.

ANGEL

And there's more to the eye than meeting me.

She finds the other part of her costume and puts it on. She doffs the shirt and keeps looking.

HAROLD

That doesn't make sense.

ANGEL

I was changing the subject. You made me nervous.

He's on to something. He knows it.

HAROLD

I made you nervous? Why?

ANGEL

Well, you almost shot me.

HAROLD

But that's not what you meant, was it?

ANGEL

I'd like to change the subject.

HAROLD

I'd like to know.

ANGEL

Why?

Now Harold gets nervous.

HAROLD

I'd like to know if it's the same reason you make me nervous.

She considers.

ANGEL

I'm smart. I don't like people to know. Men. I don't like men to know I'm smart.

HAROLD

Why?

ANGEL

Because. When they find out how smart I am, they leave.

She gets her purse.

HAROLD

That's ridiculous.

She starts to dig through it.

ANGEL

Maybe in your world. In my world they leave.

She pulls out a brush.

HAROLD

I would never leave a woman because she's smart.
How smart are you?

She points the brush at him.

ANGEL

Ah ha!

HAROLD

What?

ANGEL

Ah ha!

HAROLD

I wanted to know.

*She stands in front of the mirror, brushes her
hair.*

ANGEL

I knew it.

                    HAROLD

I was asking a question.

                    ANGEL

You can't ask that question.

                    HAROLD

Why not?

   She stops brushing and turns.

                    ANGEL

Because that's like asking what my measurements are.

                    HAROLD

I don't need to ask that. I can see that for myself.

   She turns back and starts brushing again.

                    ANGEL

Exactly. I want my men like slot machines. Just pull
the handle and make 'em spin.

                    HAROLD

You have to tell me.

                    ANGEL

Okay. Okay. Okay. I have an IQ of two hundred and
sixty.

   Harold drops into a chair.

                    HAROLD

Go on!

                    ANGEL

Documented.

HAROLD

No way!

ANGEL

It's true.

HAROLD

You're a genius.

ANGEL

Yeah. Yeah.

HAROLD

As I recall from my Laint class, the word genius comes from the word genie. And genies were the precursors to Angels in ancient mythology.

ANGEL

According to whom, Barbara Eden?

She digs around in her purse again.

HAROLD

Why this? You could be anything.

ANGEL

That is a typical academic response.

She pulls out a makeup kit, starts fixing her makeup.

ANGEL

And anyway, the word genius comes from the Latin word gignere, which means to beget.

He's back in detective mode.

> HAROLD

Which sounds mighty biblical to me. How do you—

> *He turns back to confront her suddenly.*

> HAROLD

Feel?

> ANGEL

How do you mean?

> HAROLD

It's a simple question. How do you feel? Physically?

> *She finishes her makeup, puts the kit away.*

> ANGEL

Not bad, considering my recent suicide. Where is my damn boot?

> *Again she starts looking for her missing boot.*

> HAROLD

Exactly.

> ANGEL

Exactly what?

> HAROLD

You feel fine. Me too. No hangover. No drowsiness. No unpleasant physical effects at all. Right?

> ANGEL

Unless you count waking up to you.

HAROLD

But we know that's not possible. With the amount of drugs we took, even if we survived, we should feel something. But we feel fine. Like we got a great night's sleep. Even my breath feels fresh.

ANGEL

Praise the Lord.

He peers at her closely.

HAROLD

You look good too.

ANGEL

Thanks.

HAROLD

How do I look?

ANGEL

Well...

HAROLD

Relatively I mean. Compared to yesterday.

She takes her time, walks around him, looking him over carefully.

ANGEL

Oh. Well. Good actually. Kind of glowing.

HAROLD

Exactly.

ANGEL

Maybe you're the Angel.

> HAROLD

Let's save that hypothesis for later.

> ANGEL

I'll make a note of it.

> *She starts tossing things around trying to find
> her boot.*

> HAROLD

How about mental?

> ANGEL

Yes, you seem mental to me.

> HAROLD

I mean emotionally? How do you feel? Depressed?
Angry? What is your psychological state?

> *She stops, thinks about it.*

> ANGEL

Hungry.

> HAROLD

That's not a psychological state.

> ANGEL

My stomach doesn't know that.

> *She goes to her purse again.*

> HAROLD

Exactly.

> *She digs around the purse.*

ANGEL

Stop saying that.

HAROLD

Sorry.

ANGEL

You sound like Sherlock Holmes on lithium.

HAROLD

Exactly. Sorry. But we have a mystery here. We have
to solve it.

Finally she pulls out a Twinkie.

ANGEL

Can we eat first?

HAROLD

Would Dr. Watson eat first?

ANGEL

No, but he didn't work as hard as I did.

She opens it and takes a bite.

HAROLD

Do you—

He turns back to her again suddenly.

HAROLD

Still want to kill yourself?

ANGEL

Not right now, maybe later.

She finishes the Twinkie.

HAROLD

Ex...me too. I feel...great. I feel...happy. I feel...

ANGEL

She takes out another Twinkie.

Pretty?

HAROLD

Healed. I feel Healed.

ANGEL

Can I get an amen?

He gets angry, takes the Twinkie, and points it at her.

HAROLD

This is serious. Something happened. Something important.

ANGEL

Something may have happened. What makes you think it was important?

She takes a bite of the Twinkie in his hand.

ANGEL

There's the real fallacy in your miracle theory. A miracle would never happen to us.

She digs around in her purse for more food.

HAROLD

But it did. It did. Yesterday I was suicidal. Today I am...

ANGEL

Maniacal?

*She dumps the contents of the purse on the bed
and hunts desperately for another Twinkie.*

HAROLD

Healed. I can barely remember how I felt yesterday.
It's like it was a different life.

ANGEL

Congratulations.

HAROLD

Let's do it again.

ANGEL

What? Suicide? You just got through...

*She sinks dejectedly onto the bed: There are no
more Twinkies.*

HAROLD

No. Sex. Let's make love.

ANGEL

Make up your mind. Sex or love?

HAROLD

Both?

She shakes her head.

ANGEL

You can't afford both.

He looks at himself in the mirror.

> HAROLD

Do you like me?

She looks up at him, puzzled.

> ANGEL

What does that have to do with—

> HAROLD

I've never asked anyone that before.

She looks at his reflection in the mirror.

> ANGEL

I don't know you.

> HAROLD

You're the first woman I ever committed suicide with.

> ANGEL

The world ends not with a bang but with a preposition.

Harold turns to her.

> HAROLD

Stay with me.

> ANGEL

Or should I say proposition?

He kneels.

> HAROLD

I mean it. Stay with me.

> ANGEL

Ha!

He takes her hand.

HAROLD

I'm serious.

She pulls away.

ANGEL

No.

HAROLD

Why not?

She laughs.

ANGEL

There isn't enough time in the universe to explain all the reasons.

HAROLD

There is no time. There are no reasons. All that's left is a quantum leap of faith.

ANGEL

We did that last night.

She stuffs everything back into the purse.

ANGEL

Oh I see. You think I saved you. So now you want to save me. That's sweet. And really insulting.

She heads for the door.

HAROLD

Stay with me.

She stops.

ANGEL

Stop saying that. Go back to exactly.

He goes to her, stands behind her.

HAROLD

Something happened last night. Whatever it was, I'm convinced that we can't ignore it.

He puts his hands on her shoulders.

HAROLD

We have to respect it, honor it.

She turns.

ANGEL

Forget it.

He doesn't move.

HAROLD

Okay, fine. Let's give it a moment of silence.

She puts down her purse and waits.

ANGEL

Now let's go home.

HAROLD

Yes, let's.

She picks up the purse again and starts to leave.

ANGEL

Fine.

She stops at the door.

ANGEL

What?

HAROLD

I'll leave with you.

ANGEL

No.

Gently, he takes her purse from her. She lets him.

HAROLD

Why are you here?

ANGEL

Is this a question of philosophy or location?

He puts her purse back on the dresser.

HAROLD

Yes. Why are you here?

ANGEL

It was a birthday. Or a joke. Or an accident.

She opens the door. Casino bells blast in.

ANGEL

Do you hear those bells? That's the sound of pure probability.

She slams the door closed.

ANGEL

The owners of this place can calculate to the 35th degree how much money each of those machines will make in a year.

She goes to the bucket of coins and takes out a handful.

ANGEL

Yes, you can play a dollar and take home a million. But it isn't luck, it isn't destiny, and it isn't a miracle. It's mathematics. It's probability. That's what runs the world. This world anyway. You're a physicist. You know that better than anyone.

She tosses the coins to him. They fall on the floor. One rolls to the corner.

HAROLD

That's the whole point. That's what I'm trying to tell you.

He picks up the coins.

HAROLD

Probability doesn't mean things are random. This is what they couldn't understand, at the conference.

He goes for the coin in the corner.

HAROLD

In quantum physics, we talk in probabilities, because we can't know the underlying mechanism.

He finds the coin and holds it up. It glimmers in the light.

HAROLD

Take the slot machine. You and I don't know how it works. But we know it does.

He shifts the coins from hand to hand, like a machine paying out.

HAROLD

And because probability works, we know it's not random. It's controlled. By something.

He goes back to her, at the dresser.

HAROLD

I know one thing. You're here because something brought you here. I don't know what. I don't know why.

He places the coins in her hand.

HAROLD

I'm willing to spend the rest of my life finding out. But I can't do it without you.

She drops the coins back in the bucket.

ANGEL

Stop it.

HAROLD

Why?

ANGEL

There was no miracle.

HAROLD

But we're alive.

She laughs.

                    ANGEL
We were never going to die.

                    HAROLD
The pills—

                    ANGEL
Weren't sleeping pills.

                    HAROLD
I don't understand.

She gets the purse, takes out the bottle of pills.

                    ANGEL
They were breath mints.

She takes one.

                    HAROLD
Breath mints?

She blows her breath at him.

                    ANGEL
Important part of my business.

He takes the bottle from her.

                    HAROLD
But they were in a prescription bottle.

                    ANGEL
Childproof cap. Stays closed when I have to make a quick getaway.

He tastes one.

HAROLD

Well at least that explains why my breath feels minty
fresh.

*She takes the bottle of pills, screws the cap back
on. She drops the bottle, and sees her boot under
the dresser. She retrieves it and sits on the bed to
put it on.*

HAROLD

You're leaving.

ANGEL

Yes.

HAROLD

Why?

ANGEL

It's what I do.

She starts to pull on the boot.

HAROLD

Don't.

ANGEL

First you don't want me to get undressed, now you
don't want me to get dressed.

HAROLD

Why did you have sex with me?

ANGEL

I wanted to go out with a bang?

> HAROLD

Tell me.

> *She stops.*

> ANGEL

I had to distract you until you fell asleep.

> HAROLD

I don't buy it.

> ANGEL

Someone did.

> *She pulls off the boot and throws it at him. He*
> *dodges.*

> ANGEL

Don't you know what I am?

> HAROLD

You're an Angel.

> *She laughs.*

> HAROLD

You're an Angel to me.

> ANGEL

De gustibus non disputandem est.

> *She retrieves the boot.*

> ANGEL

I was paid for, Harold.

HAROLD

No, you knew it was a mistake. I didn't pay you. You knew. But you stayed. And we made love.

She throws the boot at him, hits him this time.
He goes down.

ANGEL

We fucked, Harold. It's what I do.

She goes to him, helps him up and to the bed.

HAROLD

What does that mean? It's what I do.

ANGEL

I'm a performer. I come. I perform. I leave. I can't explain it any better than that. It's what I do.

Harold sits up in bed.

HAROLD

I remember. In the dream.

She gets some very watery ice.

ANGEL

What dream?

She wraps it in the pillowcase.

HAROLD

Maybe it wasn't a dream. Maybe it was a near death experience.

She holds it to his head.

ANGEL

You weren't near death. It was a near sex experience.

HAROLD

Whatever. I remember. It's what you do.

She takes his hand, puts it up to hold the ice.

ANGEL

What are you talking about? What dream?

HAROLD

A dream I had after...we fell asleep. You were there and I was there.

ANGEL

Was there a tin man and a cowardly lion?

HAROLD

It was an audition.

She drops the ice in his lap.

HAROLD

Ahhh! You danced. You were wonderful. So beautiful. Beautiful flowing light. You danced as if God were watching.

ANGEL

God is always watching.

HAROLD

You think so?

She looks up.

ANGEL

God I hope not.

Harold winces.

HAROLD

If he's watching, why doesn't he do something?

ANGEL

I'd have to kill you to tell you.

HAROLD

You danced like an Angel.

She gets up, moves away from him.

ANGEL

I have that dream all the time.

HAROLD

Did you have it last night?

ANGEL

Yes.

HAROLD

But something was different, wasn't it?

ANGEL

Yes.

HAROLD

It was the music.

ANGEL

I'd never heard it before.

Harold reaches over to the CD player.

HAROLD

It sounded like this.

*He turns on the CD player. Thus Spake
Zarathustra fills the room.*

HAROLD

Do you remember anything else? Any other dreams?

ANGEL

I remember you. You were teaching or something.

HAROLD

Yes. I was. Divinity school. What did I talk about?

ANGEL

You went on for an eternity.

HAROLD

Exactly.

ANGEL

You were talking about universes and dancing and...

HAROLD

Yes?

ANGEL

Miracles.

She looks at him.

ANGEL

We had the same dreams.

He nods.

ANGEL

How is that possible?

HAROLD

Miracles.

Now she is the detective.

ANGEL

It must have been the pills.

Harold blissfully counters her.

HAROLD

Breath mints.

ANGEL

The sex.

HAROLD

Spectacular. Not miraculous.

ANGEL

This is spooky.

HAROLD

Action at a distance. Exactly.

She retrieves her boot again.

ANGEL

I'm getting out of here.

HAROLD

So, you've thought this through completely, I imagine, like the intelligent woman you are, if you don't mind my using that term.

She sits to pull it on.

ANGEL

Yes. Of course. Completely. Why?

HAROLD

I know that this all seems like some accident. But it's not.

He gets up carefully and walks to the board.

HAROLD

It's a miracle. And I can prove it.

ANGEL

How?

He pauses for a moment, then erases everything.

HAROLD

How many hotel rooms are there in Las Vegas?

ANGEL

51,462.

Harold stares at her.

ANGEL

What? I haven't been in all of them. It's on the website.

He shrugs and writes 51462 on the board.

HAROLD

That means that the chance you would enter this room is 51462 to one.

ANGEL

If you say so.

HAROLD

So how long have we been in here?

ANGEL

About 5 hours?

HAROLD

Okay. 5 hours, that's 300 minutes, that's 18,000 seconds. So the chance that you would knock on my hotel door at exactly that second is—

He writes the next figures on the board too.

HAROLD

51,462 times 18,000 which is--.

ANGEL

926,326,000.

HAROLD

Right. Now, the chance that I would be on a chair with a gun at exactly the same second out of those five hours is—

He writes again.

HAROLD

926,136,000 times 18,000 which is about—

He looks at her.

ANGEL

16,670,448,000,000.

HAROLD

To one. So assuming you do this 4 times a day--

ANGEL

That's a good day.

HAROLD

300 days a year—

ANGEL

That's a good year.

HAROLD

Which is 1200 times a year, you would have to dance
for—

ANGEL

13,892,040,000.

HAROLD

Years to find someone else like me. Which is almost
exactly the amount of time since the beginning of the
universe. This is proof. This day was planned from the
beginning of the universe. It's a miracle.

He writes MIRACLE on the board and circles it.

ANGEL

You don't plan miracles.

HAROLD

You mean we don't.

She edges for the door.

ANGEL

Okay I'll agree that it's a miracle if you promise it
won't happen again for another 13 billion years.

HAROLD

Deal.

ANGEL

Look. My knocking on this door was an accident. The
fact that I did it just in time was an accident. The fact
that we're still alive is probably just...bad luck for both
of us.

He points to the board.

HAROLD

But what if it's not.

ANGEL

It is.

HAROLD

Look, I've spent my life studying accidents. That's
what quantum physics is all about.

He draws bells in the corners again.

HAROLD

But what if there really is purpose. And miracles. And
Angels.

ANGEL

And Santa Claus and the Easter Bunny.

She takes the marker from him.

ANGEL

Lives don't change because of one incident.
Tomorrow night I'll be in another hotel room with
someone else. Tomorrow night you'll be in another
hotel room shooting someone else.

HAROLD

If miracles lasted forever, they wouldn't be miracles.

She points the marker at his head.

ANGEL

Remember why you came here.

He takes the marker back.

HAROLD

I came here to meet you. Where else could I meet you?

She laughs.

ANGEL

Me?

HAROLD

I have to understand.

ANGEL

Anywhere.

HAROLD

It's what I do.

He picks up the gun.

HAROLD

You can't leave. If we go, we go together. One way or another.

ANGEL

You don't mean that.

HAROLD

Don't I?

She takes the gun.

ANGEL

No. Because there was only one bullet in the gun.

He sighs.

HAROLD

I was hoping you'd forgotten.

ANGEL

You're the kind of man who wouldn't want anyone else to get hurt by accident.

Angel puts the gun down.

ANGEL

I won't ever forget that.

He takes her hand.

HAROLD

Stay with me, Ellie.

ANGEL

Tell you what. Let's flip for it. Heads I stay, tails I go.

HAROLD

You can't be serious.

ANGEL

You wanted a test.

HAROLD

You want to decide our lives on a coin toss?

She gets a silver dollar from the bucket.

STEPHEN EVANS

> ANGEL

Look at the decisions you've made in your life.
Wouldn't you have been better off flipping a coin?

She flips the coin in the air a few times.

> HAROLD

Okay.

> ANGEL

Are you game?

> HAROLD

Do I have a choice?

> ANGEL

Do you think you do?

> HAROLD

Go ahead.

> ANGEL

Call it.

She flips the coin.

> HAROLD

Heads.

*She catches the coin and looks at it, then looks at
him.*

> HAROLD

Just one question.

> ANGEL

What?

HAROLD

How many Angels can dance on the head of a pin?

She laughs.

ANGEL

An infinite number, Harold.

She kisses him gently.

ANGEL

One after another.

Harold gets her wings from the easel.

HAROLD

You're wrong. I'm certain.

ANGEL

Certain? Why?

He hands the wings to her.

HAROLD

There is only one Angel.

*She puts her purse and wings down by the door,
then moves to the dresser to check herself in the
mirror, sees the coins in the bucket.*

ANGEL

When did you win all these coins?

Harold sits on the bed.

HAROLD

I was sitting at a slot machine, trying to decide whether to go through with it. I put a coin in. Pulled the handle. Watched the wheels. Put a coin in. Pulled the handle. Watched the wheels. And finally I thought: why should I keep playing a game I know in time I'm going to lose?

Angel takes the bucket of coins over to Harold.

ANGEL

What else is there to do in Vegas?

She walks to the door, puts on her wings, then opens the door. Casino bells blast in.

She gestures like a dealer leaving a blackjack table.

ANGEL

Good luck, Harold.

As she leaves, the door closes almost tight.

Harold sits there for a while, not knowing what to do. He picks up a coin from the bucket.

HAROLD

Heads I go after her. Tails I kill myself.

He pauses, then he puts the coin back in the bucket. He stands. Then he throws the entire bucket of coins up in the air. Coins go everywhere. When they hit the ground, Harold looks them over intently. Then he chooses one.

HAROLD

Heads it is.

He opens the door. Casino bells blast in.

HAROLD

Listen to the bells.

He rushes out. After he's gone, the CD player starts to play Thus Spake Zarathustra.

Blackout.

The End.

Stephen Evans

Playwright's Note

As our understanding (such as it is) of cosmology changes, the number assigned to the age of the universe may also change. Currently it is 13.8 billion years. In the twenty years I have been working on this play, the number has changed three or four times, to my knowledge.

If it changes again, as seems likely, feel free to change the number of hotel rooms in Vegas to make Harry's calculation come out right. Assuming it does. If I had been any good at math, I would have been a physicist myself.

About the Playwright

Stephen Evans is a playwright and the author of *The Island of Always*, *Whose Beauty is Past Change*, and *Funny Thing Is: A Guide to Understanding Comedy.*

Find him online at:

https://www.istephenevans.com/

STEPHEN EVANS

Books by Stephen Evans

Plays:

The Visitation Quartet:
   The Ghost Writer
   Monuments
   Tourists
   Spooky Action at a Distance
   At the Still Point

Experience	*Three plays about Ralph Waldo Emerson*
Generations	*(with Morey Norkin and Michael Gilles)*
As You Like It	*(by William Shakespeare, adapted by Stephen Evans)*
The Glass Door	*(An adaptation of Hedda Gabler by Henrik Ibsen)*

Non-Fiction:

Funny Thing Is:	*A Guide to Understanding Comedy*

Anthropomorphosis
Small Gifts
Liebestraum
The Laughing String: Thoughts on Writing

Fiction:

The Marriage of True Minds
The Island of Always:
The Marriage Gift
Whose Beauty is Past Change
The Mind of a Writer and other Fables
Memory Plays
Epigrammaticon
The Next Joy and the Next

Verse:

Limerosity
Limerositus
Sonets from the Chesapeke
The Crooked Mirror

www.ingramcontent.com/pod-product-compliance
Lightning Source LLC
Chambersburg PA
CBHW021645120626
46545CB00002B/711